Preparing for the Behavior-Based Interview

How to Get the Job You Want

Terry L. Fitzwater

A Crisp Fifty-Minute™ Series Book

This Fifty-Minute™ book is designed to be "read with a pencil." It is an excellent workbook for self-study as well as classroom learning. All material is copyright-protected and cannot be duplicated without permission from the publisher. *Therefore, be sure to order a copy for every training participant by contacting:*

THOMSON

COURSE TECHNOLOGY™

1-800-442-7477 • 25 Thomson Place, Boston MA • www.courseilt.com

Preparing for the Behavior-Based Interview

How to Get the Job You Want

Terry L. Fitzwater

CREDITS:

Senior Editor: **Debbie Woodbury**
Assistant Editor: **Brenda Pittsley and Charlotte Bosarge**
Production Manager: **Denise Powers**
Design: **Nicole Phillips**
Production Artist: **Zach Hooker**
Cartoonist: **Ralph Mapson**

ISBN 1-56052-643-2
Library of Congress Catalog Card Number 2001090684
Printed in Canada by Transcontinental Printing

2 3 4 5 PM 06 05

Learning Objectives For:

PREPARING FOR THE BEHAVIOR-BASED INTERVIEW

The objectives for *Preparing for the Behavior-Based Interview* are listed below. They have been developed to guide you, the reader, to the core issues covered in this book.

THE OBJECTIVES OF THIS BOOK ARE:

❑ 1) To offer insight on how to get noticed *before* the interview

❑ 2) To offer tips for interview preparation

❑ 3) To provide coaching on how to respond to interview questions

❑ 4) To explain how to ask questions that will increase your potential for job offers

❑ 5) To describe follow-up techniques that will enhance the interviewer's interest in you

ASSESSING YOUR PROGRESS

In addition to the learning objectives above, Course Technology has developed a Crisp Series **assessment** that covers the fundamental information presented in this book. A 25-item, multiple-choice and true/false questionnaire allows the reader to evaluate his or her comprehension of the subject matter. To buy the assessment and answer key, go to www.courseilt.com and search on the book title or via the assessment format, or call 1-800-442-7477.

Assessments should not be used in any employee selection process.

How to Use This Book

This *Fifty-Minute™ Series Book* is a unique, user-friendly product. As you read through the material, you will quickly experience the interactive nature of the book. There are numerous exercises, real-world case studies, and examples that invite your opinion, as well as checklists, tips, and concise summaries that reinforce your understanding of the concepts presented.

A Crisp Learning *Fifty-Minute™ Book* can be used in variety of ways. Individual self-study is one of the most common. However, many organizations use *Fifty-Minute* books for pre-study before a classroom training session. Other organizations use the books as a part of a system-wide learning program—supported by video and other media based on the content in the books. Still others work with Crisp Learning to customize the material to meet their specific needs and reflect their culture. Regardless of how it is used, we hope you will join the more than 20 million satisfied learners worldwide who have completed a *Fifty-Minute Book*.

Preface

Preparing for the Behavior-Based Interview is your guide to handling your job applications and interviews in ways that will increase your chances of being hired by your employer of choice. In this book, you'll find a step-by-step, get-that-job plan, including the initial steps of researching a company, composing and sending a cover letter and résumé, interview preparation, and anticipating and responding to behavior-based interview questions. You'll be prepared for any interview with any organization.

Terry L. Fitzwater

Terry L. Fitzwater

About the Author

Terry L. Fitzwater is a principal with Fitzwater Leadership Consulting with his principle office in California. He has authored three books in the Manager's Pocket Guide Series: *Preventing Sexual Harassment, Documenting Employee Performance,* and *Employee Relations.* He is also the author of a companion book to this one, *Behavior-Based Interviewing: Selecting the Right Person for the Job.* He is a frequent speaker and university instructor, and instructs on-site business classes in performance management, employee relations, and other topics.

He holds a bachelor's degree in business administration and a master's degree in human resources and organization development. You can contact him at 916-791-0692 or by email at tfitzh2o@quiknet.com.

Contents

Phase 4: Following Up

Appendix

INTRODUCTION

2

The Behavior-Based Interview Process

For most people the job hunting process starts something like this: Review the local newspaper for opportunities, find something interesting, fire off a résumé, sit back and *hope* to get a telephone call inviting you for an interview. While this method is effective some of the time, your goal should be to get an interview *every* time *and* increase your chances of receiving an offer of employment. This may seem like expecting too much, but it is achievable with the right level of research and preparation.

This book provides a four-phase process for developing a consistent approach to job interviews. This approach will maximize your interpersonal connection with the interviewer.

The four phases of the process are:

PHASE 1: Preparation

PHASE 2: Polishing Your Image

PHASE 3: Responding to Questions

PHASE 4: Following Up

Following these steps will help you present yourself and your skills and abilities in the best possible way. This is of prime importance because your interview time is limited. How you use the time allotted to you can make the difference between an offer of employment to you…or to the next interviewee.

As you go through the steps, you will learn:

> ➤ The importance of pre-interview research.

> ➤ Behaviors that pay off with a successful interview.

> ➤ The best responses to questions.

> ➤ What to do after the interview to encourage your selection for the job.

The Behavior-Based Interview Process (CONTINUED)

This isn't as difficult as it sounds. All it takes is a little time and practice. Most successful interviews are the result of preparation by the job candidate, especially when the interviewee rehearsed what to say and how to say it *prior* to the interview. It is no coincidence that candidates for the job of U.S. president are put through grueling "what do I say if this question is asked?" scenarios. They must expect the expected as well as the unexpected. Have you ever heard someone say, "I was lucky to get hired"? Perhaps it's true. But here is my definition of luck: Luck is where opportunity meets preparation. Keep this in mind as you read this book.

Luck is where opportunity meets preparation

Employer Objectives

Have you ever stopped to think about what the employers are trying to achieve in a job interview with you? They are trying to:

➤ gauge your skills and abilities in relation to the essential job criteria and requirements

➤ gauge your skills and abilities in relation to everyone else competing for the same job

➤ determine your level of interest in the position

➤ determine your "fit" with the unique organizational culture

➤ look at your history of success and how it applies to the organization and its current and future plans

➤ look at your history of adversity and how you matured as a result

How you meet each objective determines your likelihood of success in achieving your ultimate goal: employment. And not just any employment, but a job that is satisfying with a desirable company.

Put your best foot forward

When the unemployment rate is low, some job hunters operate under the perception that they have the luxury of picking and choosing among a plethora of available jobs. But the "warm body theory"–that is, placing unqualified or almost qualified applicants in positions just to fill them–is an accident waiting to happen for both parties. Eventually, the new employee may fail and turnover or termination is the result. No one wants to fail at an inappropriate job. And no organization desires charges of discrimination, wrongful discharge lawsuits, costly turnover, or the potential of a negligent hire. The bottom line: Even in a tight job market you need to put "your best foot forward" to win the interview race.

Behavior-Based Interviewing: Selecting the Right Person for the Job is a companion book to this one. In it, employers are trained to conduct job interviews in a way that results in finding the right person for a position, while this book assists applicants by describing a targeted approach for answering interview questions. The key to success is to understand what the interviewer is seeking.

Interview Grid

Every interview is fraught with the potential for mistakes. As an applicant, you must try to minimize this potential as a means of maximizing your candidacy. Here are eight common interview landmines and their respective remedies. Each will be discussed later in this book.

Interview Errors	Emphasizes the value of...
Lack of preparation	Research
Failure to rehearse	Practice
Not talking enough (80% rule)	Depth of response
Nonprofessional appearance	Image
Question misinterpretation	Recognition
Résumé style	Formatting
No close to the interview	Expressed interest
Lack of post-interview response	Follow up

What Are Behavior-Based Questions?

Most employers today ask only job-related questions. The reason is twofold:

> ➤ They need to determine if you fill the essential qualifications of the position.

> ➤ The only questions allowed under today's strict employment laws are those related directly to the position.

There are standard questions that most employers ask in every interview and they are the ones you should rehearse now. You know them. You've been asked them before. In preparation, think of some you know are likely to make the interview list and write them down here. Don't worry about your responses for now, as they may change as you learn this process and the importance of this word: M-A-T-T-E-R. Plan on revisiting this section later.

1. Where would you like to be in five years?

2. Why are you leaving your current employer?

Standard questions you anticipate being asked

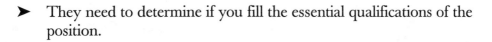

_____

_____

_____

_____

_____

_____

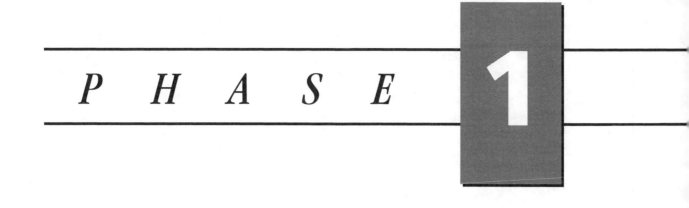

P H A S E 1

Preparation

Making a Good Initial Impression

You only have one opportunity to make a good first impression. In job hunting, this must happen before you even meet face-to-face with the hiring party. You can ensure a good initial impression that will lead to an interview opportunity through the research you do and the information you present. This includes:

➤ Investigating the company

➤ Understanding the position description

➤ Your cover letter

➤ Your résumé

Together, these elements paint a picture of the skills and qualifications an organization seeks for its vacant position. Your presentation and knowledge in each area can tip the balance between you and another applicant. Then, during the interview your job is to help the employer understand that you are exactly the person for the position.

Know your strengths to maximize your selection

Researching the Company

As you follow the instructions in this book, it will be helpful to find an advertisement for a job you'd like to have. Look in your local newspaper or on the Internet. You'll use this ad to conduct a real scenario of how to apply for the advertised position. You'll also use the ad to write a practice cover letter and revise your résumé.

The first step in preparing a job application and anticipating the interview questions is research. Check your library for past newspaper articles on the company. Call the company switchboard and ask for copies of the annual report and other public documents. And go to the company's Web site if one exists.

The Internet is a valuable resource for anyone seeking employment. Most organizations have Web pages that describe their business, the products they sell, and detail their mission and vision statements. These pages offer clues about the types of people the organization wants to hire. Many companies also have employment pages describing available positions in considerable detail. You can prepare yourself for any job application and interview by logging on and browsing the employer's Web site.

Here is a three-part mission statement taken from the Internet:

What We Do	Where We're Going	What We Believe
Our Mission is Service	Our Vision is Value	Our Commitment is People
We are a public agency providing utilities and recreation.	We seek to offer high quality services at reasonable cost	We strive to constantly improve by involving our staff, our customers, and our community.
We have a singular duty: service. Our sole purpose is to serve and stay in touch with our customers.	As we enter the 21st century, our challenge is to build value while constantly improving quality and minimizing costs.	Our vision requires the commitment of our employees. We must respect each other, honoring diversity and involving our people in decision making.

This mission statement contains a lot of information that can benefit a job seeker. Several points deal with customers, employees, quality of goods and services, and involvement of employees and customers in decision-making. If this is an accurate assessment of what the company values, it can serve the job applicant as a roadmap to the kinds of interview questions to anticipate and rehearse. Following are some examples.

Anticipated Questions

About Customers

"How would you deal with an unhappy or unsatisfied customer?"

"How would you find out if our products are what the customer needs?"

"What process would you use to solicit customer input concerning our products?"

About Employees

"We value the input of our employees. As a human resources professional, how have you demonstrated this same philosophy where you currently work?"

"How do you foster respect among the employees of your work unit?"

"How do you encourage employees to make their own decisions?"

Practice Anticipating Questions

Let's look at another example of a mission statement and a values statement, also taken from an organization's Web site.

OUR MISSION

The mission of our medical center is to promote and provide high-quality, cost-effective health care for the people in the communities we serve. Through our best efforts and collaboration with our colleagues, we strive to relieve suffering, cure illness, and promote wellness.

OUR CORE VALUES

At all times we will foster and act with integrity, encourage innovation, value relationships, show respect, be responsive, and act with fairness and consistency.

What do you see that would help you interview with this company? List and describe.

_____

_____

As a result of your research, what interview questions would you anticipate?

_____

_____

Understanding the Position Description

Most organizations have a written job description for each advertised position and are more than willing to send one prior to an interview. Standards vary, but a typical description will include the basic job function and its dimensions, plus it will outline whether the job involves supervision of others, travel, key account-abilities and responsibilities, education and experience requirements, the physical location and work environment, and other special skills, certifications, and abilities.

Use information in the job description to identify employer requirements. As an example, look at this Basic Function section of a formal job description for a mechanical engineer.

BASIC FUNCTION

This position provides technical support to the manufacturing division. The divisions are at three locations within the city of Sacramento. The position is matrixed and provides expertise to the research and development department to ensure proper instrument development.

This tells job applicants that:

➤ The position supports two organizations, manufacturing and research and development.

➤ The position requires the ability to travel to multiple locations.

➤ The individual must have experience as a mechanical engineer.

➤ Prior experience in instrument development is a plus.

As a result, you expect a certain line of questions. Here are just a few:

"Tell me about your prior experience working in an organization where manufacturing and R&D worked in conjunction with one another."

"Tell me about your technical background specifically as it pertains to instrumentation development."

Understanding the Position Description (CONTINUED)

"Did you ever have any issues where R&D and manufacturing disagreed on an approach to the manufacture of an instrument, and what did you do about it?"

"This position requires frequent travel around the city. Would this be an issue for you?"

You get the idea. The possible questions are many, but if you carefully research the job description you can be prepared for most questions.

Let's look at the key accountabilities and responsibilities section of the same job description.

KEY ACCOUNTABILITIES AND RESPONSIBILITIES:

This position requires:

✓ Development of the departmental budget

✓ Supervision of three direct and two indirect reports

✓ Ability to work with all levels of the organization

✓ Ability to conceptualize products at inception and to follow them to release

After reading this, can you guess what questions you might get in an interview?

_____

_____

_____

In section four of this book, you'll learn methods for answering the questions you develop.

Writing Your Cover Letter

The cover letter is a crucial part of the employment process. It is the first document an employer sees. Yet it often gets less careful thought and attention than it deserves, and a poorly written letter will get your résumé filed in the "round file" without further consideration. Why? Because the employer considers sentence structure, spelling, grammar, and overall presentation of material as a reflection of the applicant. Misspelled words or sentences that are nonsensical might be a symptom of someone with poor thought processes, who is careless, or who believes it is unnecessary to produce quality work. None of that is acceptable to the employer and should not be acceptable to anyone who wishes to make a good first impression during a job search.

Proof your work like your job depends on it. It does!

Objectives of the Cover Letter

A good cover letter accomplishes five objectives.

➤ It highlights your résumé.

➤ It emphasizes how your background meets the employer's advertised requirements.

➤ It points out special accomplishments that are relevant to the company.

➤ It asks for an interview.

➤ It does all this on one page.

Your goal is to produce an application that is no more than three pages: a one-page cover letter and two pages of résumé. More than that is a book and the person pre-screening résumés doesn't want to read the next great American novel in your presentation.

Let's look at an ad from Sunday's newspaper to decide how a cover letter might unfold.

Local healthcare manufacturing company needs a Director of Human Resources. The position requires at least 10 years of experience and a person comfortable in a high tech, fast-paced, high-growth organization. The ideal applicant is familiar with international employment law and capable of delivering a multitude of employee development programs. A master's degree in a business or human resources field is required.

In very few words, the ad is full of employer requirements, and most employers will tell you they do not want to review résumés if the applicant is lacking in any of the skills they desire. To see how you measure up, it is helpful to develop a grid that translates the employer's criteria into a cover letter highlighting your matching skills. Let's look at one.

Skills Grid

Advertised Needs	My Credentials
Healthcare experience	6+ years with AHS Healthcare
Manufacturing experience	3 years in manufacturing
Director level experience	Current title: Director of Human Resources
10 years in human resources	12+ years
High tech/fast pace	Knowledgeable about software and hardware
High growth	Business exceeds 20% growth per year
International familiarity	None (but AHS is international org.)
Delivering training programs	Training and organizational development experience
Master's degree	Master's degree in organizational development

This comparison accomplishes two things:

➤ It demonstrates that the applicant matches eight of the nine requested skills well enough to respond to the ad and know that the résumé will get the attention it deserves.

➤ It isolates the skills that will be emphasized in the cover letter. Using this matrix, the letter practically writes itself.

Look at the following cover letter written to target the above employer-required criteria using information from the "My Credentials" column.

Mark Jobsearch
100 Hill Road
Sacramento, CA 95825
530-546-9876
mjobsearch@ISP.com

August 6, 2002

Sandy Cheshire Smith
Recruitment Manager
Acme Healthcare
1000 Brosnan Street
San Francisco, CA 95811

Dear Ms. Smith:

I am forwarding my résumé in response to your advertisement for a <u>Director of Human Resources</u>.

Briefly, I have <u>twelve years</u> of broad human resources experience with a <u>high-tech, international healthcare</u> organization that is listed in the <u>Fortune 500</u>. AHS, named one of the best companies to work for in America, has been cited on numerous occasions for its human resource practices and innovations. I currently hold the position of <u>Director</u> of Human Resources-West for two <u>manufacturing divisions</u>. A <u>fast-paced</u> environment coupled with <u>double-digit growth</u> required strategic initiatives and unique solutions to complex change.

My experience is supplemented with considerable business acumen, an undergraduate degree in Business Administration and a <u>master's</u> in Organization Development. I have <u>developed and delivered</u> a number of programs that emphasize both business and <u>employee growth and development</u>: advanced coaching skills, performance management, positive discipline, and documentation and strategic human resource planning.

If I can provide you with any additional information, please let me know. I look forward to hearing from you.

My best regards,

Mark Jobsearch

Notice how the letter reflects the Skills Grid. Each item from the grid is under-lined to demonstrate to you how to work the employer's requirements into the text. Any employer reading the letter can easily determine that the writer matches a number of the required qualifications and will want to read the résumé as a result.

Now look at another advertisement. Circle the key words you would emphasize to the employer.

> TLF, a Fortune 100 company with an international presence, seeks a Vice President of Sales. The person must have at least 12 years of sales experience, with five years in senior management. Experience in France and the Benelux countries is a plus. This position reports directly to the President and is responsible for the management of more than 400 sales representatives.

Practice Creating a Skills Grid

Make a list of your own skills that you want to feature in your job search.

_____

_____

_____

_____

Now, use your skills list to make a Skills Grid for the ad you found earlier. Draft a practice cover letter on a separate sheet of paper. When you're finished, move on to next section where you'll take a look at your résumé.

Skills Grid

Advertised Needs	My Credentials

Developing Your Résumé

Most job advertisements garner numerous responses. As a result, your résumé exists for one reason: to help *you* stand out from the crowd. Your chances improve if your résumé meets the advertised criteria and:

- ➤ explains your career objective

- ➤ shows chronologically the organizations where you have been employed

- ➤ presents a clear picture of the positions you have held

- ➤ outlines your accomplishments

- ➤ details your education and skill sets

Are any of these more important than another? Not really. But the Skills Grid combined with your preparation and research might lead you to emphasize particular attributes. For example, if an advertisement begins with "Ph.D. required," it's an obvious hint to highlight that accomplishment. Likewise, if your research leads you to the conclusion that experience in a specific area will be highly valued, e.g., high tech, you will want to highlight it in both your résumé and your cover letter.

As a career-minded professional who is job searching, you probably have a résumé on file. But is it up to date? Do you evaluate it occasionally to see if it can be improved to increase its effectiveness? Do you have different versions that give a higher profile to specific skills? Do you tailor it every time you send it to an employer? Taking these steps will ensure a résumé that is more likely to get you in the door for an interview.

At minimum, a professional-looking résumé must:

- ➤ be clean and crisp with proper spacing and margins

- ➤ be grammatically correct

- ➤ detail your skills and accomplishments

- ➤ be to the point and kept to a maximum of two pages

Sell yourself with detailed brevity, not a dissertation

Résumé Elements

Review the following sample résumé. The key elements are discussed in more detail in the pages to follow.

Gregg Miller
1000 Alhambra   916-291-7903 HM
Granite Bay, CA 95746   916-231-0713 WK

Objective: To continue career progression and personal development through growth opportunities with innovative organizations.

Employment History:

1996 to Present   **FLC-The Performance Management Company**
                Senior Human Resource Consultant

Provide consulting services with a focus on organizational change and strategic human resource planning, including mergers, acquisitions, divestiture due diligence, and organization development with an emphasis on restructuring, team formation, and core competency development. Focus on employee relations programs such as coaching, non-punitive discipline, conflict and complaint resolution, opinion surveys, 360-degree feedback, performance management, harassment prevention and investigation, and other employment-related issues.

Key Accomplishments:

➤   Developed and installed a non-punitive discipline system/program for a 3000-employee division of a Fortune 200 organization.

➤   Developed a harassment prevention program and delivered the product to all employees of a large, networked organization.

1979 to 1996   Factor, Inc.
                Vice President of Human Resources

Executive leadership team member responsible for formulating strategy and directing global human resource activities for three divisions and managing employee relations for global business operations. Sites were fully integrated and included sales, marketing, distribution, customer service, finance, quality assurance, research and development, software and hardware engineering and design, and information technology.

Key Accomplishments:

➤ Restructured the domestic and international businesses to align synergies.

➤ Redesigned the management development process for strategic human resource planning.

➤ Managed due diligence for the acquisition and divestiture process relating to policies, practices, procedures, compensation and benefits and employee relations.

➤ Blueprinted the management process for strategic reengineering.

➤ Managed all employee relations and employment law issues including union avoidance, harassment prevention and all matters pertaining to charges of discrimination and/or wrongful discharge issues.

Cola Inc.
Personnel Manager

Human resource generalist responsibility for corporate research and development, engineering, and three pilot manufacturing plants.

Food Co.
Human Resources Manager

Human resource generalist responsibility for two food processing plants with a total employee population of 1500.

Education:

University of South Florida
College of Business Administration
Major: Management

University of San Francisco
College of Professional Studies
Major: Human Resources and Organization

Elements of an Effective Résumé

The sample meets most of the initial goals of an effective résumé. Use this checklist to develop or revise your own résumé.

- ❏ Explains career objective (or includes a Statement of Objectives)

- ❏ Chronologically lists each former employer (Work History)

- ❏ Presents a clear picture of all positions held

- ❏ Outlines skills and accomplishments with broad-brush statements and bullets

- ❏ Lists any technical skills and credentials

- ❏ Details education

- ❏ Appears clean and crisp with proper spacing and margins

- ❏ Grammatically correct

- ❏ Kept to one or two pages

A detailed list of each element is provided on the following pages.

Career Objective

A career objective is a succinct statement positioned at the top of your résumé. Any statement of more than two sentences is too long. To be effective, the career objective must:

➤ catch the reader's attention

➤ suggest why you are applying for the position

Basically, it clarifies why you are a good fit for the job opening at their company. You may wish to create a general objective, then tailor it to individual employers every time you submit an application.

Let's take a look at two distinct career objectives:

Objective: To apply my existing human resources skills working for a company known for innovative human resources policies, and to continue my personal development by reaching for new responsibilities in the areas of employee training and retention.

Objective: To combine my fluency in written and verbal Japanese with my background in technical manufacturing, providing translation and quality control for an international company known for its breakthrough designs and programming.

Practice Writing Objectives

Reread the advertisement you used to write a practice cover letter. Use the following space to develop a career objective for the résumé you would submit to that employer.

Objective: _____

_____

_____

Elements of an Effective Résumé (CONTINUED)

Statement of Qualifications

As an alternative to a Career Objective, you can begin a résumé with a Statement of Qualifications. This is a brief summary of the skills you would bring to the hiring organization. Let's look at an example for clarification.

Statement of Qualifications: Fluency in written and verbal Japanese combined with a bachelor's degree in business and four year's experience in technical manufacturing. Background includes technical writing for international clients.

Practice Writing a Statement of Qualifications

Look back to the Skills Grid you developed earlier. It details the items you should highlight when developing a Statement of Qualifications. Use the grid to develop your statement in the following space.

Statement of Qualifications: _____

_____

_____

Chronological Work History/Positions Held

Hiring authorities want to know where you worked and what you did there. This is usually the meat of the résumé. Traditionally, a professional résumé also included how long you worked at each organization, but this is something you may want to reconsider today.

Should you include dates of employment on your résumé? The issue is that dates give the reader a clue as to your age. Even though any organization will tell you it does not discriminate on the basis of age, some do, even subconsciously. A solution is to include the dates of employment for the position you currently hold and not for the others. However, if age—whether you'll be perceived as too old or too young—is not an issue for you, feel free to detail the dates of employment for each job.

Age is also an issue when you document your educational history. No one needs to know when you graduated, only that you did.

Review the past positions listed on your résumé. Do you want to keep the dates? It's a good idea to keep a record of the dates on one copy so that you can always put them in when they're needed. Whether using dates or not, make sure the positions are listed chronologically beginning with the most recent. Always include the name of the company and your job titles.

Elements of an Effective Résumé (CONTINUED)

Outline of Accomplishments

Each of the jobs listed in your Work History should be accompanied by a short paragraph that gives a broad-brush description of your essential job duties for the positions held. This is the time to "blow your own horn."

Think of times when you saved your employer money, developed new or improved procedures, trained others, proposed new or improved products, brought in a new technology, trained workers independently or as part of a team, and so on.

Broad-Brush Description

Here is an example of a broad-brush description for an editor who worked at Acme Publications for five years:

1997-Present
Associate Editor for *Extra!* Magazine
Acme Publications

Primary liaison with all contributing writers and photographers for weekly magazine covering breaking political news. Administer contracts and licensing agreements, coordinate with section editors, and schedule production work. Conduct fact checking and supplementary writing in a high-paced, quality-driven environment.

In addition to the broad-brush description, bullet points are a smart way to emphasize major accomplishments. A key to writing effective bullet points is to begin each sentence with an action verb. Action verbs command attention and add instant credibility to your skills portfolio.

Action verbs add instant credibility

Here is a list of action verbs. Look at the sample résumé to see the words used in context. A list of action verb statements is also included in the Appendix.

Analyzed	Established	Produced
Challenged	Exercised	Provided
Controlled	Expanded	Redesigned
Coordinated	Facilitated	Reduced
Created	Implemented	Resolved
Delivered	Improved	Restructured
Demonstrated	Increased	Strategized
Designed	Managed	Supervised
Developed	Orchestrated	Targeted
Directed	Organized	

Bullets with Action Verbs

Here are a couple of bullet points for the editor from Acme Publications.

➤ Restructured editorial calendar to provide additional proofreading time and reduced incidence of errors by 50%.

➤ Expanded stable of writers to acquire regular contributions from experts in key subject areas.

Take a look at your résumé and rewrite your broad-brush descriptions and bullet points as necessary using action verbs.

Elements of an Effective Résumé (CONTINUED)

Technical Skills

In addition to your job history, employers today often want to know that you have experience with the technology used to do the job. Include information on the computer software and hardware you have used, machinery you can operate, special permits or training you have received.

The technical skills portion of your résumé can look like this:

> ## TECHNICAL SKILLS AND CREDENTIALS:
>
> Strong Windows knowledge, including use of database, word-processing, and customer contact programs.
>
> Certified Public Account.

Educational Background

Your résumé should conclude with a section on your educational background. It is a good practice to mention the schools attended, your major, and any degrees conferred. There is no need to mention grade point averages or school activities. Most employers only want to know if you have the requisite degree. If they require additional information they will probe for it in a telephone pre-screening or during the interview.

Here's one way to display and describe educational background:

EDUCATION:

University of South Florida
BS—College of Business Administration
Major: Management

University of San Francisco
MS—College of Professional Studies
Major: Human Resources and Organization Development

Your final product—a job application that gets noticed—should be a cover letter and résumé, together no more than three pages. If developed properly, your presentation will encourage the hiring authority to move on to the next step: inviting you to an interview.

34

Polishing

Your Image

The P-A-R Technique

First impressions have magnified importance in a short interview. Hence the thought, "What they see is what they think they get."

Appearance

If the interviewer is introduced to someone with an unkempt appearance— wrinkled clothes, unruly hair, scruffy shoes—or to someone dressed inappropriately for the position—trendy street clothes in a conservative corporate environment—the candidate's true talents may be overlooked. People do judge books by their covers. The way to get the full benefit from an interview is to show the interviewer you are prepared on the outside as well as the inside. Always dress for the occasion. A suit or dress is usually in order, even at a company that promotes casual dress.

Your company research can help you know what to wear. If possible, get advice from someone who works there.

In addition to a professional appearance, two other factors help garner a favorable first impression: poise and rapport. Here is a good way to remember all three. Think of the word **P-A-R**.

Poise

Appearance

Rapport

The P-A-R Technique (CONTINUED)

Poise

Poise is important, but what is it? Here's the definition from Merriam-Webster's dictionary:

> "Poise — easy self-possessed assurance of manner : gracious tact in coping or handling, also : the pleasantly tranquil interaction between persons of poise…
> **b** : a particular way of carrying oneself."

In the initial meeting, expect the interviewer to "break the ice" prior to beginning the formal interview. This may include an exchange of pleasantries, an offer of a cup of coffee or a soft drink, questions about your trip to the facility, etc. Why? To give you time to adjust to the environment and to give you an opportunity to calm down. If you are like most people, you will be a little nervous. This is natural. Don't expect to be Mr. or Ms. Cool. This is your time to display poise under pressure and it gives you the opportunity to collect yourself. Take advantage of the time and keep in mind Webster's definition.

What should you do during this period? Here is a checklist. Remember it as you prepare for any interview.

- ❏ Calm down. Gain control of your emotions or nervousness.

- ❏ Introduce yourself with confidence born from your experience.

- ❏ Reach out first for a firm (not Herculean) handshake.

- ❏ Take a seat when it is offered.

- ❏ Answer the ice-breaker questions thoroughly. It will help to ease anxiety and get you ready for the interviewer's job-related questions.

Rapport

If you have used the poise checklist, you are well on your way to making a good first impression. But here is something important to remember: Job offers are sometimes won or lost because of inadequate relationship skills. This is especially true if the position requires interaction with a variety of individuals, departments, and organizational levels.

Good relationship skills can be demonstrated by establishing a positive rapport with the interviewer. To meet this goal, you should:

❏   Make regular eye contact

❏   Show a friendly and cordial demeanor

❏   Express thanks for being invited to an interview

❏   Expand on areas of mutual interest introduced by the interviewer, such as sports, books, and so on.

The P-A-R-T-N-E-R Technique

Your ultimate goal as an interviewee is to P-A-R-T-N-E-R with the interviewer. Partnering, by definition, is a collaboration of effort. You can go further toward building your positive image with a mutually rewarding exchange of information. Let's take P-A-R to the next step with this concept.

Poise

Appearance

Rapport

Thoroughness of response

Note your surroundings

Express yourself clearly

Reflect on the good and the not so good

Thoroughness of Response

This involves letting your stream of consciousness bring you to your answer naturally. Never sell yourself short with too short answers. Interviewers want to hear responses that answer every aspect of a question. Image is built through communication and a complete, concise, well thought-out answer will put you in a more favorable light.

➤ Think before you respond

➤ Respond in detail

Note Your Surroundings

It is easier to build a positive image and rapport if you can find common areas of interest with the interviewer. While most interviewers will not admit to biases, all have them. Upon entering the interviewer's office, note the pictures, posters, photographs, or degrees on the wall. Look for signs of hobbies, favorite vacation spots, and so on. Use any theme to your advantage by mentioning that you too went to "State U," or your last vacation was in Hawaii, or that you also display pictures of your favorite golf course.

Express Yourself Clearly

Interviewers are impressed by those who detail their qualifications in an articulate manner. Language usage is a measure of intelligence *and* education. Use it to your advantage to enhance your image with the interviewer. Avoid repetitive phrases such as "you know" and space fillers such as "um." Use complete sentences.

➤ Choose your words carefully

➤ State your sentences clearly

Reflect on the Good and the Not So Good

Honest answers will enhance your image. Not every work situation you've experienced was favorable. Not every performance review was outstanding. If you are asked about these kinds of situations, answer them honestly. If they were positive say so; if not, say that, too, but cautiously. You'll be given some pointers in the next chapters for answering these kinds of tough questions.

TIP: Know that you will dominate the conversation by doing approximately 80% of the talking. This is expected, so do not hesitate to take all the time you need to explain your skills and abilities and why you are the best person for the job. The interviewer has a limited amount of time to analyze whether you can do the job, so maximize that effort with detailed responses.

42

PHASE 3

Responding to Questions

44

Taking Center Stage

This is where it all comes together. Your preparation and research, your well-written cover letter and résumé, *got you noticed*. Your appearance and introductions made a positive first impression. Now it is time to secure a job offer by using your interview answers to demonstrate your understanding of the position and that you have what is required to be successful.

Rehearsal

You'll be more successful in any interview if you rehearse first. In real estate, the tried-and-true axiom is "location, location, location." In interviewing, it's "rehearse, rehearse, rehearse." This chapter tells you what to rehearse. Several rehearsal techniques include:

➤ Watching yourself in the mirror.

➤ Recording your responses so that you can play them back and listen to your answers and voice inflections.

➤ Staging a mock interview with a friend. Have someone else critique your answers, mannerisms, eye contact, tone, and so on.

Types of Questions

The anagram M-A-T-T-E-R will help you remember that most interview questions fall into six categories.

Type of Question	What the interviewer wants to know
Motivation	What gets/keeps you excited about your work?
Ambition	Where do you want to go in your career?
Technical	What technical skills do you bring to the job?
Theoretical	What if...?
Energy	What keeps you going each day?
Relationships	How do you fit within the organization, its culture, and its mix of people?

Have you ever been in an interview where you asked the person to restate the question because you did not understand it? The simple reason may have been that you were unable to classify it. If you learn to identify the type of questions asked, you will increase your chance of responding appropriately—without hesitation and in detail. Let's look at what interviewers are seeking and the meaning behind M-A-T-T-E-R.

Motivation

These questions try to discover what excites you about your work or keeps you satisfied. In today's climate of self-directed teams and multi-tasking, most organizations want individuals who are self-motivated and do not require daily supervision.

Ambition

These questions seek to determine whether you are likely to progress within the company once you are hired. It is important to demonstrate upward mobility since most organizations do not look for people who will be satisfied with the status quo. Remember, an organization cannot survive without succession planning and you need to appear to be the person who will move up because of your desire and abilities.

Technical

These questions are the easiest to identify. They concern the actual skills you bring with you, not just current experience in the field. Expect to be quizzed on your credentials, education, professional affiliation, and familiarity with technology.

Theoretical

These questions are the most difficult because they deal with the hypothetical. They often start with phrases such as "Let's suppose...." or "Let me describe a situation for you...." or "How would you handle...?" The purpose of these questions is to evaluate creativity, attitude, past situational experience, and to see how well you think on your feet.

Energy

Organizations are looking for employees who run, not walk, to task completion. Demonstrate energy through animation, enthusiasm, and by describing tasks you completed efficiently or even ahead of time.

Relationships

These questions seek to determine how well you get along with people. Here are some examples.

"How well did you get along with your former supervisor?"

"Tell me about a time you disagreed with someone."

"How would you rate the people you work with?"

"Tell me about a time you had a disagreement with a co-worker."

The purpose is to determine temperament, how well you work and problem solve with others, and how long it might take you to assimilate into the organization.

CATAGORIZING QUESTIONS

A question may M-A-T-T-E-R in more ways than one. That is, a question may be part relational and part motivational. Now that you know the types of questions you will be asked, see if you can identify real questions using M-A-T-T-E-R.

1. How do you keep yourself apprised of the latest technologies in your field of expertise?

   ❏ Motivation   ❏ Theoretical

   ❏ Ambition   ❏ Energy

   ❏ Technical   ❏ Relationships

2. How well did you get along with your last supervisor?

   ❏ Motivation   ❏ Theoretical

   ❏ Ambition   ❏ Energy

   ❏ Technical   ❏ Relationships

3. Let's create a hypothetical situation. How would you convince a key supplier to lower its prices?

   ❏ Motivation   ❏ Theoretical

   ❏ Ambition   ❏ Energy

   ❏ Technical   ❏ Relationships

4. What kind of work do you really like to do?

   ❏ Motivation   ❏ Theoretical

   ❏ Ambition   ❏ Energy

   ❏ Technical   ❏ Relationships

CONTINUED

5. What does a normal work day look like for you?

- ❏ Motivation
- ❏ Ambition
- ❏ Technical
- ❏ Theoretical
- ❏ Energy
- ❏ Relationships

6. What kind of a job do you see yourself in next year?

- ❏ Motivation
- ❏ Ambition
- ❏ Technical
- ❏ Theoretical
- ❏ Energy
- ❏ Relationships

Answer Key: 1. Technical/Ambition, 2. Relationships, 3. Theoretical, 4. Motivation/Theoretical, 5. Energy, 6. Motivation/Ambition

)ose of Questions

terview question has a purpose. Your best chance at a solid response
om preparation and your ability to display certain characteristics associ-
ι each type of question in the M-A-T-T-E-R anagram.

M-A-T-T-E-R **Give them the answers they're looking for**

Motivation Provide examples of the internal satisfaction you get from
teamwork or seeing a task through to completion.

Ambition Mention examples of past upward mobility, a willingness to
relocate for a good opportunity, or desire to learn new tasks and
skills.

Technical Demonstrate a working knowledge of your area of expertise and
how you maintain currency in your chosen field including
continuing education, professional memberships, etc.

Theoretical Show a rational thought process that flows logically from start
to finish and incorporates a positive attitude.

Energy Be interested and enthusiastic, not only regarding the specific
topic but also in terms of how you can be a part of furthering
the concepts being discussed.

Relationships Let the interviewer see your concern for past and present relationships and your willingness to always be a part of the solution and not the problem. Downplay conflicts as "business, not
personal," and as constructive and proactive.

A key to a successful interview is to reflect on your own style, needs, and requirements in advance, so that you'll be prepared to answer the questions that M-A-T-T-
E-R. Your ability to relate these personal elements to the interviewer is of supreme
importance. The interviewer must see and hear them in order to give you proper
consideration. Start preparing with the What's the M-A-T-T-E-R? grid.

What's the M-A-T-T-E-R?

M-A-T-T-E-R	Examples	Your experience
Motivation	Challenging work, new tasks, working with people	What motivates you? 1. 2. 3.
Ambition and goals	Steady advancement, increased responsibility, complete master's degree	What are your aspirations? 1. 2. 3.
Technical skills	Certifications, degrees, honors, recognitions, special training	What skills and credentials do you bring to the position? 1. 2. 3.
Theoretical	Unique situations and/or experiences	Describe situations where you succeeded or failed in past jobs and how you gained from the experience. 1. 2. 3.
Energy	Active displays of energy and enthusiasm	How will you demonstrate enthusiasm? 1. 2. 3.
Relationships	Well liked by co-workers, served on committees, active in community events	What situations can you describe to demonstrate professional relationships? 1. 2. 3.

Pet Questions

Every interviewer has pet questions, and fortunately for the job seeker, most ask the same pet questions of every candidate, making it easy for you to prepare and rehearse. Some of these questions will not be job-related, but will be informative to the interviewer. The bottom line: Answer them as you would any other question—with confidence based on your past results and accomplishments.

When answering pet questions, remember to first identify them with M-A-T-T-E-R. Review the following list of pet questions and indicate which type they are by checking (✔) the appropriate box(es).

1. Where do you want to be five years from now?

   ❏ Motivation   ❏ Theoretical

   ❏ Ambition   ❏ Energy

   ❏ Technical   ❏ Relationships

2. Why do you wish to leave your current employer?

   ❏ Motivation   ❏ Theoretical

   ❏ Ambition   ❏ Energy

   ❏ Technical   ❏ Relationships

3. What do you like best about your current employer? Why?

   ❏ Motivation   ❏ Theoretical

   ❏ Ambition   ❏ Energy

   ❏ Technical   ❏ Relationships

4. What do you like least about your current employer? Why?

   ❏ Motivation   ❏ Theoretical

   ❏ Ambition   ❏ Energy

   ❏ Technical   ❏ Relationships

5. What are your top three greatest skills or strengths?

    ❏ Motivation   ❏ Theoretical

    ❏ Ambition   ❏ Energy

    ❏ Technical   ❏ Relationships

6. What are your developmental needs?

    ❏ Motivation   ❏ Theoretical

    ❏ Ambition   ❏ Energy

    ❏ Technical   ❏ Relationships

7. What do you like best about your current supervisor?

    ❏ Motivation   ❏ Theoretical

    ❏ Ambition   ❏ Energy

    ❏ Technical   ❏ Relationships

8. What do you like least about your current supervisor?

    ❏ Motivation   ❏ Theoretical

    ❏ Ambition   ❏ Energy

    ❏ Technical   ❏ Relationships

9. Tell me what you think you can contribute to our organization.

    ❏ Motivation   ❏ Theoretical

    ❏ Ambition   ❏ Energy

    ❏ Technical   ❏ Relationships

10. Tell me about the specifics of your last performance review and why you agreed or disagreed with its contents.

    ❏ Motivation   ❏ Theoretical

    ❏ Ambition   ❏ Energy

    ❏ Technical   ❏ Relationships

Pet Questions (CONTINUED)

11. If I were to ask your employer about your performance, what do you think he or she would say?

- ❏ Motivation
- ❏ Ambition
- ❏ Technical

- ❏ Theoretical
- ❏ Energy
- ❏ Relationships

12. If I were to ask your employees about your management style, what do you think they would say?

- ❏ Motivation
- ❏ Ambition
- ❏ Technical

- ❏ Theoretical
- ❏ Energy
- ❏ Relationships

Answer Key: 1. Motivation/Ambition, 2. Motivation/Ambition, 3. Relationships, 4. Relationships, 5. Technical/Energy, 6. Ambition/Technical/Theoretical, 7. Relationships, 8. Relationships, 9. Ambition/Technical/Theoretical, 10. Relationships, 11. Technical/Relationships, 12. Relationships

The Positive Approach

The first question in the list of Pet Questions concerns your motivation and your ambitions. You know that the interviewer is looking for a response that demonstrates both what motivates you to complete tasks and your aspirations for upward mobility. The interviewer also may be probing your willingness to relocate for opportunity, as well as your desire to learn new tasks and skills. Use your answers from the What's the M-A-T-T-E-R? grid and you'll have a solid response to the question all ready.

Here's what your answer might look like:

1. Where do you want to be five years from now?

I have always been motivated by challenges. In that regard, I am never satisfied with the status quo. I embrace the concept that change often leads to improvement.

Over the years, my results have led to me being promoted on several occasions. I started as a sales representative and within two years was promoted to a sales manager and within another year was promoted to district sales manager. Each promotion required me to learn a new set of skills and I attended three training programs to develop supervisory skills and to learn how to read my P&L to make sure I fully understand my financial obligations to the bottom line of the business.

To continue my development, I am currently attending a course to learn how to better motivate and mentor the employees who report to me. I believe it is important to develop the next set of managers. My last promotion, by the way, required that I relocate and I was more than willing to do so to advance.

You can see how a response flows once you understand what is behind the question. Let's look at a response to Pet Question number seven. Keep in mind the question is attempting to determine how you value relationships.

7. What do you like best about your current supervisor?

My current supervisor has been a mentor for me especially as it pertains to my ability to coach and mentor those employees who report to me. He leads by example in that he continually demonstrates the value of on-going communications and does so with an interactive leadership style. In both regards, I constantly try to mirror the style because it is a very effective way to lead. He always asks for input and is always available to help if I need it.

The "Positive Twist" Approach

All questions should be answered in a positive manner wherever possible. Even when the reality of a situation may have been less than positive, you should try to find positive aspects and emphasize those. Never lie, but downplay negative disagreements. For example, if you generally disagreed with everything your supervisor said or did, you should not say "I am just glad to be out from under her. She was completely clueless about how to run a department."

Instead, you should consider, "My supervisor and I did not always agree on every issue nor did we totally agree on the direction the department should take each and every time. However, after voicing my opinions, if she decided to go in a certain direction, I would always work toward the success of that direction."

Turning negatives into positive experiences will always enhance your image. This type of response does three things:

➤ It solidifies your role as a team player.

➤ It shows that you are willing to implement ideas different from your own.

➤ It demonstrates a willingness on your part to actively yet diplomatically disagree on direction.

It is a good rule to always look for and state the positive in any situation. Now try it for Pet Question number two.

2. Why do you wish to leave your current employer?

Remember, this is a motivation/ambition question. Look back at the What's the M-A-T-T-E-R? grid to review your answers regarding what motivates you and your ambitions.

Now write a response to the question:

_____

_____

_____

_____

_____

_____

Behavior Evaluation Criteria

Expect to be evaluated on five to ten behavioral criteria. Behavioral criteria are defined as the *actual skill requirements* for the position in question. Who determines the criteria? The interviewer. The criteria are defined by his or her research using such sources as job descriptions, performance reviews, and interviews with employees who hold, or have held, the job. It is much of the same information you have learned to gather as part of your job search.

It is necessary to be familiar with each criterion so you can prepare appropriate responses. Let's look at 20 criteria typically used in the interview process. Each one is followed by four suggestions to help you think about a logical response. This takes time, but the effort will result in detailed and complete interview answers that will impress any interviewer. As you review each criterion, write any ideas that come to mind in the space provided, no matter how trivial. These initial thoughts will assist when the time comes to fill in details.

Criteria: Time Management

The optimum use of time to maximize your efforts and that of others

➤ Describe projects you have delivered on time.

➤ Describe how you prioritize projects to ensure completion.

➤ List classes you have taken to become more proficient.

➤ Describe a project that was late and how your efforts brought it back under control.

_____

_____

_____

_____

_____

_____

Behavior Evaluation Criteria (CONTINUED)

Criteria: Risk Taking

Viewing failure as an opportunity for growth despite personal risk or exposure to criticism

➤ Describe a new technology and how you adapted it to your work.

➤ Describe your thought process on determining if a risk is worth taking.

➤ Describe a situation where you were rewarded for taking a risk.

➤ Describe a situation where you were not supported, but took the risk anyway.

_____

_____

_____

_____

_____

_____

Criteria: Learning Capacity

The ability to absorb and adapt new technology to the existing environment

➤ Describe a new technology and how you learned to use it.

➤ List and describe continuing training and development courses.

➤ Catalog your strengths.

➤ List past positions and technologies you had to learn to become effective.

_____

_____

_____

_____

_____

Criteria: Decision Making

The ability to make timely, quality decisions, not necessarily with all the necessary information

➤ Describe the thought process you use to make a decision.

➤ Detail the results of an important decision that you made leading to increased effectiveness or profitability.

➤ Characterize how you involve others in decision making and why.

➤ Describe a situation where a decision you made was not supported and the process you used to gain support.

_____

_____

_____

_____

_____

_____

Criteria: Leadership

Demonstrating by example, the willingness to be out in front

➤ Describe a situation where your leadership skills or style helped bring about a successful conclusion.

➤ Develop a list of descriptive words to describe your leadership capabilities or style, such as "tenacious," "open to feedback," "willing to work with others," "willing to challenge the status quo," etc.

➤ Describe a difficult project and what you did to select talent, plan the project, overcome obstacles, etc.

➤ Describe a situation where you took "hits" because of your desire to finish a task.

_____

_____

_____

_____

_____

Behavior Evaluation Criteria (CONTINUED)

Criteria: Interpersonal Skills

The ability to relate, communicate, or empathize at all organization levels

➤ Describe your predominant style with others.

➤ Describe how you work with teams or in meeting situations.

➤ Develop a list of five interpersonal skills that best describe you, e.g., easy to communicate with, look to others for opinions and ideas, etc.

➤ Describe a situation where you disagreed with someone and what you did ease the tenseness of the situation.

_____

_____

_____

_____

_____

_____

Criteria: Training Associates

The ability to teach or coach the skills needed to accomplish goals and tasks

➤ Describe how you determine the skills of a key team member and how you develop those skills.

➤ Describe a situation where you knew a person needed training and what you did to get them the training.

➤ Describe training you have presented to others.

➤ Describe the success of several people reporting to you as a result of your development efforts.

_____

_____

_____

_____

_____

Criteria: Oral Presentation Skills

The ability to present ideas logically and influence others verbally

➤ Describe the last two presentations you made before groups, the topic, ideas   presented, results, etc.

➤ Describe the process you use to put together important presentations.

➤ Describe a presentation you made to gain support for a project and the successful adoption of the project as a result.

➤ Describe a situation where you convinced others to adopt your position.

_____

_____

_____

_____

_____

_____

Criteria: Written Skills

The ability to present ideas logically and influence others through a written format

➤ Inventory any manuals you have written and that are currently in use.

➤ Describe the process you use to write a letter or memo.

➤ Describe any writing courses you have attended.

➤ Describe a time where you had to write a difficult letter to your work group and the positive results.

_____

_____

_____

_____

_____

Behavior Evaluation Criteria (CONTINUED)

Criteria: Managing Change

Views and welcomes change as necessary for people and organizational growth

➤ Describe new systems or technologies you have installed in your work group.

➤ Describe a difficult work issue. e.g. downsizing. and how you worked with your group to ease the transition.

➤ Describe a new technology that you are considering and why you believe it will help your department/company.

➤ Describe a time where the culture needed to change and what you did to support the change.

_____

_____

_____

_____

_____

Criteria: Technical Skills

The required knowledge, expertise, and skills for the position, task, or function

➤ Describe all continuing education efforts on your part to stay current in your field of expertise.

➤ Describe your "strengths" in your field.

➤ Describe any unique expertise you bring to the position.

➤ Describe a situation where your expertise was needed to resolve the issue.

_____

_____

_____

_____

_____

_____

Criteria: Results Orientation

Delivers tasks and assignments on time, every time

➤ Describe projects that you delivered on schedule.

➤ Explain what "results" means to you.

➤ Describe the process you use to set goals and how you achieve them.

➤ Describe the previous year's goals and how you attained them.

_____

_____

_____

_____

_____

_____

Criteria: Planning and Organization Skills

Using time management and project oversight to ensure optimal results

➤ Describe the process you use to prioritize and plan your work.

➤ Detail past projects and how you organized the work, the people, and other resources to accomplish the objective.

➤ Describe how you deal with unexpected work assignments and how you manage to achieve the desired results.

➤ Develop a list of five plans you accomplished.

_____

_____

_____

_____

_____

Behavior Evaluation Criteria (CONTINUED)

Criteria: Delegation Skills

The assignment of tasks and objectives to staff

➤ Describe the process you use to assign work to others.

➤ Tell how a staff member was promoted as a result of your effective delegation.

➤ Describe a crisis and how you resolved the issue by delegating to others.

➤ Describe the advantages and disadvantages of delegation.

_____

_____

_____

_____

_____

Criteria: Coaching

Continual, constructive feedback and advice

➤ Describe a situation where you needed to coach an individual and the positive results of your efforts.

➤ Describe the thought process you use to determine when coaching is needed.

➤ Explain why you think coaching is a workplace necessity.

➤ Outline a difficult coaching assignment and how it led to the successful "turnaround" of the employee.

_____

_____

_____

_____

_____

Criteria: Strategic Thinking

The continual assessment of the future for business application and potential

➤ Detail a strategic plan and how you aligned the department objectives to meet the plan goals.

➤ Describe new and emerging technologies and how the organization would benefit from adopting the concepts.

➤ Detail your vision five years in the future.

➤ Detail how you stay abreast of emerging trends.

_____

_____

_____

_____

_____

_____

Criteria: Mentoring

To guide and direct for the purpose of development

➤ Describe a time when you effectively coached someone to improve performance.

➤ Describe a person you thought was underutilized and how you changed the situation.

➤ Describe any mentoring programs you developed or helped to develop.

➤ Describe why you think mentoring is important to individual development.

_____

_____

_____

_____

_____

_____

Behavior Evaluation Criteria (CONTINUED)

Criteria: Business Acumen

Understanding the interconnectedness of business functions

➤ Describe your financial understanding of the entire business.

➤ Describe any situations where you served on cross-functional teams.

➤ Describe any assignments in areas other than your own.

➤ Detail emerging technologies and their use within your department and the business.

_____

_____

_____

_____

_____

Criteria: General Management and Thought Process

Skills related to and applied to organizational savvy

➤ Describe your current management style and why it is effective.

➤ Describe management positions you have held and what each contributed to your current management skill set.

➤ Detail examples of methodologies you changed or added to improve a work process.

➤ Describe how you organized your department or a project to increase overall effectiveness.

_____

_____

_____

_____

_____

Criteria: Customer Orientation

Understanding the importance of internal and external customer relations

➤ Recount customer focus groups you worked with and how they changed your assumptions.

➤ Describe your efforts to provide or improve customer service.

➤ Detail a situation where you assisted a less than satisfied customer and how those efforts resulted in the customer's satisfaction.

➤ Describe your customer-service philosophy.

_____

_____

_____

_____

_____

_____

Problem Identification

The ability to discern issues creating difficult interpersonal or organizational situations

➤ Detail how you react to problematic situations and the process you use to resolve them.

➤ Detail a problem you have encountered and how you resolved it.

➤ Detail a difficult organizational issue, such as termination or harassment, and your role in recognizing and resolving the conflict.

➤ Detail how you discern if an issue needs others involved to resolve it.

_____

_____

_____

_____

_____

_____

68

P H A S E 4

Following Up

Closing the Interview

How you close the interview is as important as your responses. Virtually every interviewer will end the session by asking if you have any questions for them. Don't pass up this opportunity to further demonstrate your interest in the company and the position. Come prepared with some closing questions and try to save at least one of them for this moment. This will demonstrate that you:

➤ prepared for the interview

➤ are interested in the organization

➤ established a rapport with the interviewer

➤ have knowledge about the organization

➤ understand the position

Your closing questions should be designed to gather more information about career potential and the employer's expectations and plans.

Sample Questions to Ask Potential Employers

"How can I make an immediate contribution to the organization?"

"If you could rank the success factors needed for this position what would they be?"

"What two or three things could the person you hire do immediately to have a positive impact on the business?"

"How does the position strategically fit into the future plans of the business?"

"What would be the logical progress from this position?"

See the Appendix for more suggestions.

Response Options

The interview is over. What do you do now and when do you do it?

First, it is common courtesy to thank the interviewer for their time and reiterate that you are interested in the position. Basically, there are three ways to communicate this to the interviewer. You can write a letter, send an email, or you can telephone the person.

Telephone

Begin by eliminating the telephone option. Understand that interviewers are usually very busy people. If they accepted telephone calls from everyone they interviewed, they would never have the time to interview in the first place. As nice as it sounds to speak to someone with whom you may have formed a bond, do not do it unless the interviewer specifically asked you to do so.

Email

This is a good option in today's market. Most employers want computer literate employees and this method demonstrates that you have at least some computer literacy. You will know if the company welcomes this option by looking at the interviewer's business card. If there is an email address, go ahead and use it.

Letter

The traditional method of writing a letter is a tried-and-true option that can be coupled with an email. You can mail the letter after sending it over email. When choosing this course, consider adding a postscript to the email noting, "Hard copy to follow." This should not be viewed as overkill, but rather as a safeguard against lost email.

Writing a Follow-Up Letter

The letter is your final opportunity to make a good impression. Therefore, like its cover letter counterpart, it should be:

➤ grammatically correct

➤ neat in appearance

➤ concise

➤ free of errors

Your letter should state:

➤ your interest in the position

➤ your appreciation for the interviewer's time

➤ your conclusions on why you are a good fit for the position

➤ additional information you may not have discussed related to the opportunity

➤ your contact information

Like your initial cover letter, this one should be no longer than a single page. And don't forget: *always run a spell check*. On the next page is a sample thank-you letter.

74

January 15, 2002

William Smith
Vice President of Human Resources
The XYZ Institute
1000 Miami Blvd.
Miami, FL 33916

Dear Bill:

Thank you for the opportunity to interview with you
and the others involved in the process. I very much
appreciated the time Ken Doe, Glenn Fitzwater, and
Sarah Jones spent with me discussing my candidacy for
the Director of Engineering position.

I would like you to know that I have thought about your
opportunity and I am interested in pursuing it
further. Based upon your description of the position,
my education, and my unique experience in Hyper
Thruster technology, I feel I could contribute
immediately to your program and the company as it
continues to be a leader in this field. You might also like
to know that I am attending a special conference in two
weeks to cover a new feature of Hyper Thruster technology. I know it will add to my expertise and knowledge
of the field.

Please call me at your convenience to discuss the next
step. You can reach me at 916-784-0692.

Again, it was my pleasure to meet you and I thank you
for your consideration. I want this job, and look forward
to hearing from you.

My best regards,

Kathy Kline
Senior Design Engineer

COMPOSING A FOLLOW-UP LETTER

You have just interviewed for an opportunity to use your area of expertise with Saddlecreek Ltd. You interviewed with two individuals, Phillip Lightfoot and Steve Clements. You forgot to mention in the interviews that you are trained in computer-assisted modeling techniques. You are also leaving immediately for a two-week vacation, but want the interviewer to know you can be reached at the Paradise Hotel at 888-648-1249. Draft a letter of thanks for your interview.

Date

Regular Business Addressing

Salutation

Introduction

thanks

Continuing

fit, and additional information

Contact information

Ask for the job

Final Checklist

Preparing for a behavior-based interview takes time and effort. But the time invested could be the difference between a job offer and a reject letter. Preparation is not a substitute for actual skills, but it will put those skills in a favorable light *every* time. As you review the final checklist, remember to Rehearse! Rehearse! Rehearse!

Did you...

- ❏ Conduct research to anticipate employer questions?

- ❏ Develop your Skills Grid?

- ❏ Write a cover letter referencing employer requirements?

- ❏ Develop a résumé using broad-brush statements and action verbs?

- ❏ Keep the cover letter and résumé to three pages or less?

- ❏ Plan for the use of P-A-R-T-N-E-R to enhance your image?

- ❏ Use M-A-T-T-E-R to increase your opportunity to make reasoned, applicable responses?

- ❏ Rehearse your responses to anticipated employer questions?

- ❏ Anticipate a list of pet questions and develop answers for them?

- ❏ Write your follow-up letter to the employer?

- ❏ Double check grammar, spelling, sentence structure, etc. on all the above?

A P P E N D I X

Internet Resources

The Internet hosts a number of job search sites. To visit them, choose your favorite search engine and type in the words "job search sites." Here is a list of the kinds of sites you will find.

ajb.dni.us

careerbuilder.com

careercity.com

careerlab.com

careermag.com

careersjournals.com

cweb.com

dice.com

employsearch.com

globecareers.com

headhunter.net

hotjobs.com

job.com

kforce.com

monster.com

nationjob.com

résumésafari.com

review.com

Action Verb Statements

Here is a list of phrases you can use to bullet-point your résumé. Use these phrases as ideas to assist you in developing your own list of accomplishments. As you read through them, remember your goal is to highlight your accomplishments, not to explain each bullet point in detail. Any interviewer interested in discussing these further will ask for clarification in the interview. Try combining the ideas presented here to personalize your document.

Analyzed negative sales variances and reduced cash outflows by 55%.

Assessed XYZ's technology potential and gained support of the executive team to invest $9 million in new product development.

Challenged our forecasting techniques and reduced report preparation time by 10 hours a month as a result.

Controlled overhead expenses and reduced total cash outlay by 22%.

Coordinated the divestiture process for the sales of a major business segment.

Created the Opportunity for Continuous Improvement Committee, increasing employee input into the operation of the business.

Created a highly profitable independent subsidiary by integrating two business segments into one viable business.

Demonstrated a 12% staff-time reduction through process re-engineering.

Designed a new instrument for the diagnoses of infectious diseases and received a patent for the design.

Directed the activity of 30 team members to resolve operational issues negatively impacting the manufacturing department.

Directed 20 operators, technicians, and engineers to complete contract negotiations ahead of schedule and $4 million under plan.

Developed and installed a non-punitive discipline system to proactively impact negative work behaviors before they became problematic.

Developed, planned, and managed two cost-cutting automation tools from inception to implementation.

Developed a synergistic leadership team and won the Excellence in Operations Award in 1998 and 1999.

Established a customer service group to proactively increase customer input and to quickly resolve complaints.

Established in-house instrument service capability saving $3 million in previously outsourced dollars annually.

Expanded international sales from $1.5 million to $25 million resulting in profitability within two years.

Facilitated several vice presidential level meetings to strategize the next budget and our expansion into new markets.

Facilitated a team from three departments to create twenty-five new design practices.

Redesigned the management development process for strategic human resource planning.

Reduced customer complaints by 50% by establishing a program to follow up on complaints within 24 hours of their receipt.

Managed the XYZ project, bringing it in on time and within approved budget allocations.

Managed a task force to create and implement computer programs to reduce span time 45% and cut man-hours 60% for proposal design analysis.

Optimized the design of a new product, bringing it in under plan and on time.

Restructured domestic operations to properly align all business segments resulting in increased business efficiencies.

Supervised a staff of twenty sales representatives to plan over-achievement of 20%.

Questions to Ask the Interviewer

The best questions to ask are those that give the interviewer an opportunity to describe the business, the position, or other circumstances that lead to success in the position. They will also help you to understand what you are getting yourself into and whether you feel this is the job for you.

Asking questions demonstrates interest on your part, so don't be shy. However, you should limit your questions to five or seven. This is your time to find out about the company, not conduct another interview.

Selected Questions

1. How would you describe the overall structure of the organization?
2. What is the structure of the department where I will work?
3. What is the predominant management style of the business?
4. What are the five most important business issues facing the organization?
5. What are the five most important objectives facing the department where I will work?
6. What interpersonal skills are needed to be successful?
7. What can I do to have immediate positive impact?
8. Will future product expansions require updating my current skills?
9. Will future business expansions require updating my current skills?
10. What other departments will I work with?
11. Can you share with me any strategic initiatives planned or underway?
12. Can you describe my expected contributions to those initiatives?

Make your own additions to this list:

_____

_____

_____

_____

Additional Reading

Ball, Frederick W. and Barbara B. Ball *Killer Interviews*. NY: McGraw Hill, 1996.

Berk, Diane. *Preparing for Your Interview*. Boston, MA: Course Technology/ Thomson Learning, 1990.

Bloch, Deborah P. *Have a Winning Job Interview*. Learningworks, 1997.

Byham, William C. with Debra Pickett. *Landing the Job you Want: How to Have the Best Job Interview of Your Life*. Three Rivers Press, 1999.

Fitzwater, Terry. *Behavior-Based Interviewing*. Boston, MA: Course Technology/ Thomson Learning, 1998.

Jackson, Tom. *Interview Express*. Time Books, 1993.

Kay, Andrea. *Interview Strategies That Will Get You the Job You Want*. Betterway Publications, 1996.

Lamplugh, Rich. *Job Search That Works*. Boston, MA: Course Technology/ Thomson Learning, 1991.

Mahony, Marchy. *Strategic Resumes*. Boston, MA: Course Technology/Thomson Learning, 1992.

Marker, Patty and Jan Bailey Mattia. *Job Interviews Made Easy*. VBM Career Horizons, 1995.

Straub, Carrie. *jobsearch.net*. Boston, MA: Course Technology/Thomson Learning, 1998.

Toropov, Brandon. *Last Minute Cover Letters*. Franklin Lakes, NJ: Career Press, 1998.

NOTES

NOTES

NOTES

Now Available From

Books•Videos•CD-ROMs•Computer-Based Training Products

Subject Areas Include:

Management
Human Resources
Communication Skills
Personal Development
Sales/Marketing
Finance
Coaching and Mentoring
Customer Service/Quality
Small Business and Entrepreneurship
Training
Life Planning
Writing